EK KADAM

KISI KE SANG EK KADAM

DR. RAVI RAZZ(CEO AND FOUNDER)

Copyright © Dr. Ravi Razz(ceo And Founder)
All Rights Reserved.

This book has been published with all efforts taken to make the material error-free after the consent of the author. However, the author and the publisher do not assume and hereby disclaim any liability to any party for any loss, damage, or disruption caused by errors or omissions, whether such errors or omissions result from negligence, accident, or any other cause.

While every effort has been made to avoid any mistake or omission, this publication is being sold on the condition and understanding that neither the author nor the publishers or printers would be liable in any manner to any person by reason of any mistake or omission in this publication or for any action taken or omitted to be taken or advice rendered or accepted on the basis of this work. For any defect in printing or binding the publishers will be liable only to replace the defective copy by another copy of this work then available.

Contents

Prologue

Ek Kadam

@Minorstudy_poetry

@Minorstudy_poetry

U hi aise ush ka waqt badla ki,
Akela rah kar maut se dosti kar li

Duniya se dur rahne ki zid karne lagi,
Toh kabhi khwabo se baate karni lagi

@Minorstudy _poetry

@Minorstudy_poetry

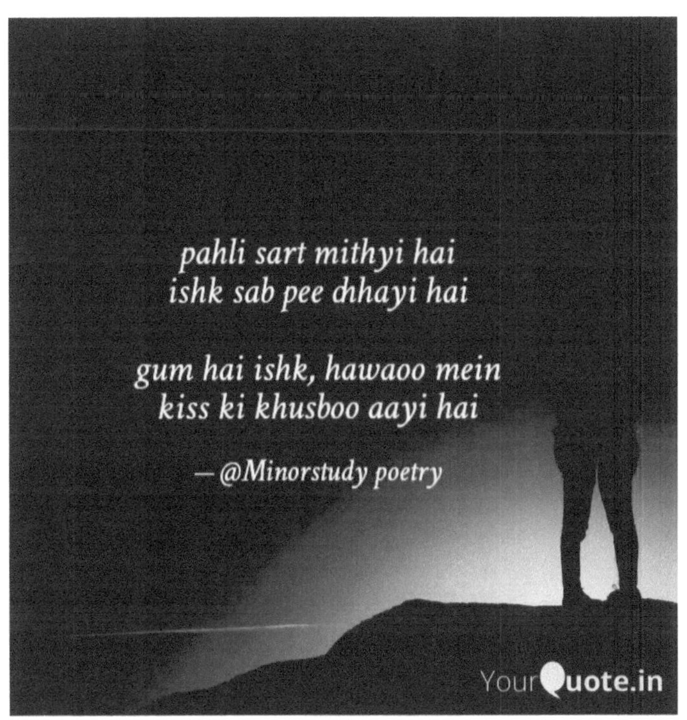

@Minorstudy_poetry

@Minorstudy_poetry

@Minorstudy_poetry

chalti phirti hai, hawaoo mein nami
chalo hum bhi, paidal chalte phirte hai

pyash sadiyoo ki, aankhoo mein liye
Chalo hum bhi kahi chalte phirte hai

— *@Minorstudy poetry*

@Minorstudy_poetry

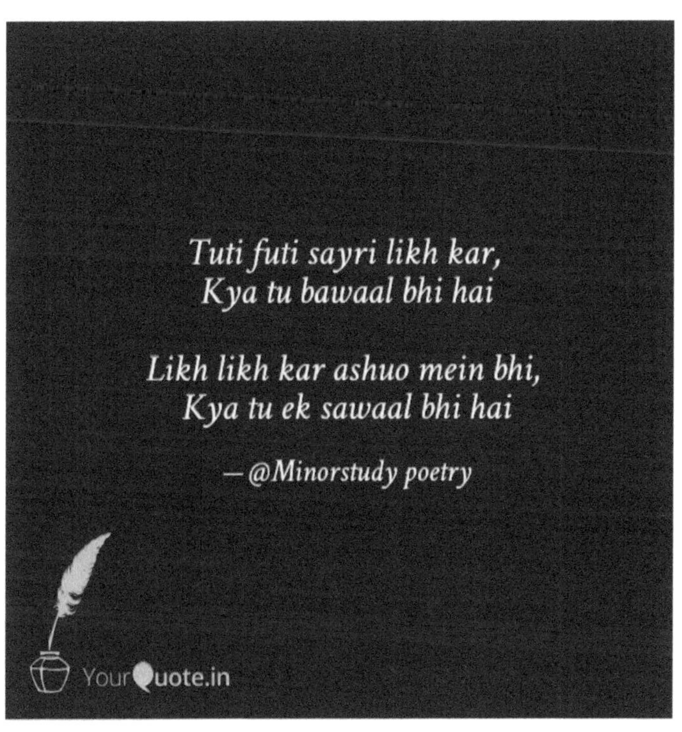

@Minorstudy_poetry

@Minorstudy_poetry

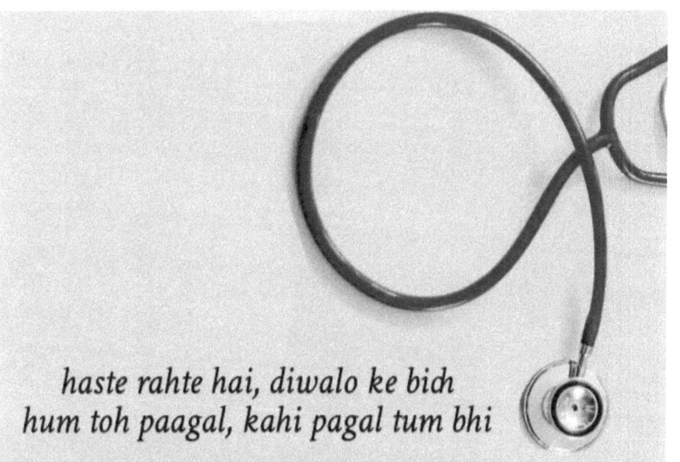

@Minorstudy_poetry

@Minorstudy_poetry

Dil ki baati bujhi aur
nazar pahuchi phir meri

kha! kha! kha!
karoge jaan kar kya?

— @Minorstudy poetry

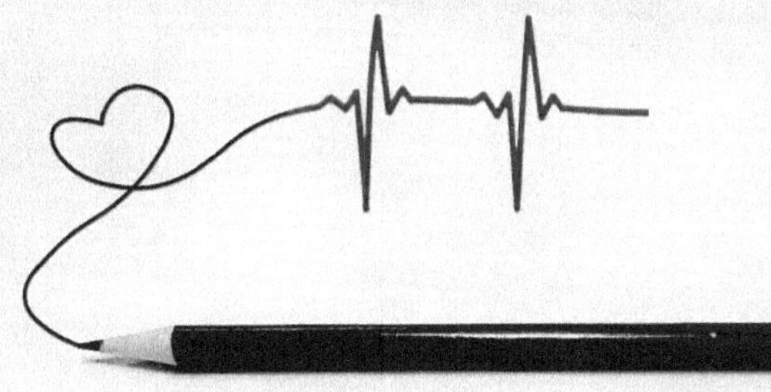

@Minorstudy_poetry

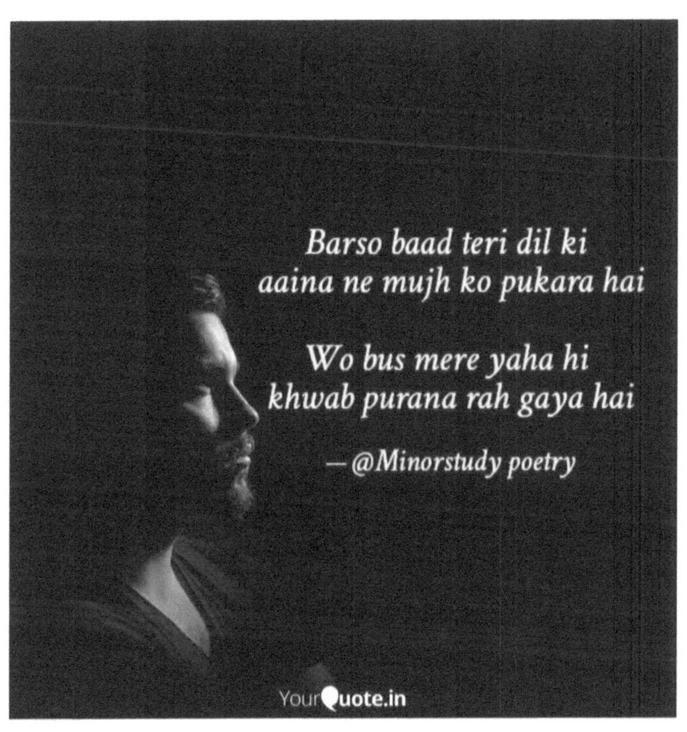

@Minorstudy_poetry

www.ingramcontent.com/pod-product-compliance
Lightning Source LLC
Chambersburg PA
CBHW061410160726
47995CB00002B/551